David was a brave, young man who looked after his father's sheep.

He protected his sheep from a fierce lion.

He did this with God's help.

David was musical too. He sang and played the harp.

Samuel poured oil on David to show that God wanted him to be king one day.

David went to visit his brothers who were soldiers fighting the Philistines.

Only David would fight the giant, Goliath. David knew God would help him.

He picked up some stones from the brook and got his sling ready.

David hit Goliath on the forehead and he fell to the ground.

David became the hero of the country. Women sang songs about him. However, the King of Israel, King Saul, became jealous.

Saul tried to kill David by throwing a spear at him. David dodged it twice.

Jonathan, Saul's son, was a great friend to David.

He helped him to escape from Saul.

David had
to hide
in a cave.
Many
joined him.
God kept
David safe.

David was crowned King of Judah, then later over all Israel.

David lived in Jerusalem. He had the ark of the covenant brought there. He worshipped God.

David wanted to build a house for God, but because he had been a man of war, God did not allow him to do this.

David trusted in the Lord. We must too.

For God sent his son, Jesus, to save sinners.